The Buz'Gem Blues

The Buz'Gem Blues

Drew Hayden Taylor

Talonbooks

2002

Talonbooks
P.O. Box 2076, Vancouver, British Columbia, Canada V6B 3S3
www.talonbooks.com

Typeset in New Baskerville and printed and bound in Canada.

Third Printing: September 2006

The publisher gratefully acknowledges the financial support of the
Canada Council for the Arts; the Government of Canada through the
Book Publishing Industry Development Program; and the Province of
British Columbia through the British Columbia Arts Council for our
publishing activities.

National Library of Canada Cataloguing in Publication Data

Taylor, Drew Hayden, 1962-
   The buz'gem blues

   A play.
   ISBN 0-88922-462-5
   I. Title.
PS8589.A885B89 2002   C812'.54   C2002-910060-7
PR9199.3.T35B89 2002

ISBN-10: 0-88922-462-5
ISBN-13: 978-0-88922-462-9

The Buz'Gem Blues premiered at the Lighthouse Festival Theatre in Port Dover, Ontario on July 4, 2001 with the following cast and crew:

PROFESSOR SAVAGE . . . . Terry Barna
MARIANNE. . . . . Columpa C. Bobb
AMOS . . . . Ian Ferguson
THE WARRIOR WHO NEVER SLEEPS . . . . Tim Hill
MARTHA. . . . . Lee Maracle
SUMMER. . . . . Kirsten Van Ritzen

Directed by Janet Amos
Set Designer: Bill Chesney
Lighting Designer: Sandra Marcroft
Costume Designer: Jocelyne Sobeski
Production Manager: Simon Joynes

Foreword

The Buz'Gem Blues is the continuing story of a set of characters I happen to bump into in several earlier plays. Martha and Marianne Kakina are refugees from the first play in this series, *The Bootlegger Blues*. Amos and Summer joined the fun during the creation of *The Baby Blues*, part two in the anticipated quartet of plays I like to call "The Blues Quartet." *Buz'Gem* is the third, and obviously the fourth has yet to be written but the ideas are already percolating all through my noggin.

The purpose of this play was twofold—in my travels I would notice a kind of reverence, almost hero worship of the Elders in our communities. While acknowledging that our Elders are incredibly important to us, it made me wonder if by putting them on pedestals, it made them seem less grounded in some way. Also, the idea of Elders dating or how Elders develop romantic relationships seem to be such a foreign concept to us non-Elder types, that I felt obligated to investigate such a topic dramatically. Thus was born *The Buz'Gem Blues*.

The second reason was part of my constant attempt to highlight and celebrate the fabulous aboriginal sense of humour. In our zeal as writers, some of us have tended to explore the darker side of First Nations existence, to illustrate and document the tragedies and their continuing repercussions in our communities. When an oppressed people get their voice back, they tend to write about being oppressed. But, a Blood Elder was once quoted as saying

"Humour is the WD-40 of healing." So consider yourself oiled.

In this series of plays, I try to take the audience, both Native and non-Native, on a fun-loving and enjoyable trip into the hearts of our communities. I try to show the humour in our lives, the craziness that sometimes happens, and the sudden twists and turns that can happen to people who happen to be Native. Everybody's welcome.

However I would like to point out that even though this is a play written by a Native writer, taking place at a Native Elder's conference, with a primarily Native cast and dealing with Native issues, it is surprisingly cross-cultural. Because, I assure you, true humour is universal. There is no unique way for a Native person to boil an egg, nor is there a particularly distinctive manner for a Native woman to love her child, and while I may say that we do have a special sense of humour, it is one that is easily appreciated and accepted by all. A Kraft Dinner joke is a Kraft Dinner joke in any culture.

The joy of writing this play was the opportunity to revisit some old friends, create some romantic sparks and see the kind of mischief a can of Spam can create. For if you can't enjoy the work you do, the friends you meet (or make), then there's not much point in being a writer, now is there?

Drew Hayden Taylor
October 2001

Acknowledgements

As with any project of love and hard work, there are several important people I must thank for adding their unique essence to the book you now hold in your hands. First and foremost, the lovely Janet Amos for her hard work, clever ideas, and rollicking laughter that let me know I was heading in the right direction. I hope she had as much fun as we did!

A special ch'meegwetch to Isadore Toulouse, who as before with other projects, helped me with the Ojibway translations in this book. I cannot possibly forget the cast of this production and the various workshops we had during its long development, your DNA is on it as much as mine (but don't expect child support).

Robert More and the amazing powers behind him at Port Dover's Lighthouse Festival Theatre who allowed me to recreate the fun and magic of the Blues series and give it a home. You guys (and gals) ain't seen nothin' yet.

And on a more personal note, to Dawn T. Maracle, who supplied the emotional and spiritual support to explore the boundaries of Ojibway/Mohawk relationships, its many bounties and surprises. Also, may thanks to Randy Reinholz, Jean Bruce Scott, Native Voices and the Trinity Repertory Theatre.

And my highest and most heartfelt thank you goes out to my mother and all the Elders out there who have so much to teach us, and yet have so much fun in their hearts. They were and are my inspiration. In a perfect world, I'd love to buy them and the world a can of Spam ... read the play, you'll get the joke.

ACT ONE

Scene One

PROFESSOR THOMAS SAVAGE walks across the stage to a large podium where he stops and faces the audience in a scholarly manner. He addresses the audience as if he were giving a paper to a group of fellow colleagues. Behind him is a big screen for overhead projections. In his hand he has a clicker to change slides.

SAVAGE

The Canadian Aboriginal. I'm sure you know one. Maybe several. They may live in your community. They may date somebody you know. They may even work where you work. They drive cars, order pizza, have their clothes dry-cleaned. They are every where. Once thought of as the "vanishing Indian," they are thriving. But what do we really know about them?

He clicks the clicker once and a picture of a Native man appears, a kind of fun picture.

SAVAGE

This is a Native person. Study him for a moment if you will. Tonight's lecture will be the first in a series where I will be taking you on a journey into the deepest, darkest part of aboriginal society. A place few non-Natives have dared to tread. It is a place of only rumours and conjecture, of mystery and adventure. It has taken me many years to build their trust and confidence but finally, I will be able to complete my research about these fascinating people. For as luck would have it, this weekend, an Aboriginal Elders' Conference will be taking place at this very university. With the raw data I will be able to collect from the series of interviews I plan, I will finally be able to present to you, my trusted colleagues, my ground-breaking report in this series of lectures.

He clicks again and the title of the report appears.

SAVAGE
"An In-depth Analysis of the Courting, Love, and Sexual Habits of the Contemporary First Nations People as Perceived by Western Society. Volume One."

SAVAGE clicks it again.

SAVAGE
Or "The Natives are Restless" by Professor Thomas K. Savage.

Scene Two

A typical commons room in a university, set up for a gathering. MARIANNE enters, carrying several suitcases.

MARIANNE

(*takes a deep breath*) I can almost smell the education. I always wanted to go to university. I think I would have made a good student, if people weren't so preoccupied with good grades. What do you say, Mom?

MARTHA enters behind her.

MARTHA

Why does everything in the white man's world have to have so many steps?

MARIANNE

The doctor told you to get more exercise. That was only one flight. We got to get you in shape, Mom. Life begins at sixty. That's what *Chatelaine* says.

MARTHA

Well good for her, whoever she is. I just want to sit down and rest my weary bones. Look at this place. I'm telling you Marianne, I still don't feel good about this thing you dragged me to. It's not me.

MARIANNE

It's an Elders' conference. You're an Elder. It is so you.

MARTHA

But I've never been into all this sweetgrass-waving, tobacco-burning, walking-around-things-clockwise silliness. I'm a good Christian woman. I don't know what I have to do with all these goings on. Besides, I'm missing my soaps.

MARIANNE

You speak the language, Mom. That's why you're here. There's a whole series of workshops on just language alone. You just have to be there and be yourself.

MARTHA

I just have to stand there and talk, and they'll pay me for that? What do I have to say?

MARIANNE

Whatever you want. Just be yourself. Just be natural. Just be Ojibway.

MARTHA

Just be natural and myself, huh? Do I get extra money if I breathe too? Ojibways do that too, you know. Goodness, my parents could have made a lot of money at these things. When I was young, the government tried beating the language out of us. Now they're payin' us to speak it. I just wish them white people would make up their minds. So what do we do now? Want me to say something in Indian? Aabiish teg zaaki-moogaming? (Where's the washroom?)

MARIANNE

That would be the door with the picture of the woman on it.

MARTHA

Wait a couple seconds and I'll do something really natural. I wonder how much that pays?

MARTHA disappears inside a washroom as MARIANNE wanders about the room.

MARIANNE

Hey Mom, did you hear? Miss Indian World is supposed to be here at the conference too. She's the one from that pageant they hold down in

Albuquerque. I hear part of that competition is that you have to demonstrate some talent related to your Nation. Rumour has it she's Seminole from Florida and she wrestled an alligator to win. Gotta admit, that's a hard act to follow. I'd always thought about entering it myself but I don't think they consider bingo a traditional talent.

MARTHA exits the washroom, drying her hands.

MARTHA

I'm sorry. You say something?

MARIANNE

No. Not me. Never. Nobody listens to me.

MARTHA

When you have something worth listening to, I do. David listened to you too.

MARIANNE

Shh. David is not to be mentioned on this trip. He does not exist anymore. He is a ghost. A non-person. That's why we came here together, remember? Mother-daughter stuff. I'm through with men. But who knows Mom, maybe we can hook you up with somebody.

MARTHA

You must have me confused with another mother. I don't want a new man. The one I had for twenty-nine years was just fine.

MARIANNE

Good attitude. The less men the better. Just the girls. I know you liked David. I liked David. We had eleven good years together but times change. But that's done. I want to start over again. A brand new Marianne and a brand new life. No turning back.

MARTHA
But Marianne, David lives right beside us.

MARIANNE
Andrew and Angie should have that window bricked up by now.

MARTHA
You work together at the Band Office.

MARIANNE
He's in finance, I'm in membership. Different parts of the building completely. Look, Mom, I don't want to talk about this anymore. I have to heal. That's why I arranged this trip.

MARTHA
We have to travel a hundred miles for you to heal?

MARIANNE
It's the old falling-off-the-horse metaphor.

MARTHA
These days, just make sure you have a saddle.
Marianne, sometimes I worry about you.

MARIANNE
Thanks Mom but I'm a grown girl now.

MARTHA
Not to your mother.

THE WARRIOR WHO NEVER SLEEPS appears, complete with dark shades, looking ultra-Indian. He is wearing a Mountie coat. Before entering, he lets out a warrior yell which startles the two women.

WARRIOR
Ahneen, she:kon, tansi, kwe kwe, boozhoo.

MARIANNE
Geez, my heart! Why did you yell like that?

WARRIOR
I was greeting the spirits of the room and honouring
your presence.

MARIANNE
A handshake would have been good enough.

WARRIOR
Are you Marianne and Martha Kakina?

MARIANNE
That's us. The Judds of the Native Community.

WARRIOR
Then I am your helper. Welcome to the Elders'
conference. I am the Warrior Who Never Sleeps.

MARIANNE
I … I'm sorry. What was that name again?

WARRIOR
I am the Warrior Who Never Sleeps. This is the name I
have chosen.

MARIANNE
Why?

WARRIOR
I have taken a vow that until our people are free, our
customs respected, our culture honoured, I will be the
Warrior Who Never Sleeps.

MARIANNE
Well, good for you. Mom, meet the Warrior Who Never
Sleeps. This is the Mother Who Always Says "I Told You
so," Martha Kakina.

WARRIOR
Our conference is blessed by your presence.

MARTHA
Can you see out of those glasses?

17

WARRIOR
My vision is all encompassing, never ending, and sharp like the gaze of our brother, the mighty eagle.

MARTHA
(*to MARIANNE*) Did he say his mother was a mighty beagle?

MARIANNE
As a matter of fact he did. Well, Warrior boy, it's been a long drive and I was told we had a room or something somewhere. Can your eagle eyes take us there?

WARRIOR
Yes, the Elder must rest. Her journey was long.

MARIANNE
Excuse me, but I'm the one who drove the whole way here. She slept most of the trip.

MARTHA
Shh, don't bother the boy. Let him respect his Elders.

WARRIOR
Do you have any more luggage?

MARIANNE
Just some emotional baggage from my childhood ... Lead the way, Warrior Who Never Sleeps. I don't suppose you ever met my ex-husband, the Warrior Who Never Puts the Toilet Seat Down?

They exit.

Scene Three

In the cafeteria, AMOS is chopping vegetables. SUMMER enters, carrying a tray covered by a dishtowel.

SUMMER

Amos, do you think that you became a cook largely because Mohawks, as part of the larger Iroquoian tradition, are matriarchal, meaning of course that you are rebelling against the commonly held Western cliché of the woman belonging in the kitchen?

AMOS

Sure.

SUMMER

Or do you think you developed your culinary skills because of the gregarious nature of the aboriginal culture, having to do with the ancient Indigenous tradition of making sure your guests never leave hungry? Sort of an anthropological dinner party ethic?

AMOS

I don't know. I wish I did, Summer but I don't.

SUMMER

It isn't that difficult a question.

AMOS

Summer, I became a cook because I like food—making it, eating it. I like making people happy by serving it to them. And, I'm doing this because I'm getting paid. It's a great motivator.

SUMMER

That's not very spiritual or ethno-based.

AMOS

Where do you get these words?

SUMMER
> I'm just trying to get to know you better, both as a man and as a Mohawk. If the two can be separated.

AMOS
> Of course they can. You don't have to be a man to be a Mohawk. Ask my sister.

SUMMER
> Your sister doesn't like me.

AMOS
> She doesn't know you. She also has that Reserve mentality where you don't trust anybody over twenty-five who doesn't have at least two kids.

SUMMER
> Do you want children?

AMOS
> I have five already, remember?

SUMMER
> I know. Three are older than me. And four of them don't like me either. I meant, do you want children with me?

AMOS
> I'm sixty-one years old. You'd end up diapering the both of us.

SUMMER
> I'm beginning to wonder if I am meant to follow this path.

AMOS
> Which path?

SUMMER
> My path with you. A search for my aboriginal knowledge. To find my place in the community.

AMOS

Why do you always get these crises just before a major contract? Summer, you are who you are. I know you have questions. I have questions. The day we stop asking questions is the day we die. But you are treating your questions as a weakness. They are there to give you strength in your journey. You will find your answers, not by being upset, but by keeping your eyes and ears open for the answers.

SUMMER

I just sometimes wonder if, maybe, I'm Mohawk.

AMOS

You ask that everyday, my sweetness, and like I said, someday, the Creator will give you an answer. Until then, you're an assistant cook. A very special one. That's a big responsibility in the Haudenosone community. How's your pastry coming along?

SUMMER

You always know how to perk me up. Keep in mind, I've never done this before.

AMOS

Looks lovely. What do you call it?

SUMMER

A chokecherry parfait.

AMOS

Smells great too. I think it's a lovely idea, you wanting to combine traditional aboriginal ingredients and contemporary foods.

SUMMER

Well, since I am one sixty-fourth aboriginal, Mohawk or not. And as such, a hybrid, I feel it is truly part of my destiny to bring the foods of both cultures. Spending the summer on the Pow wow trail in your food stand taught me the need for more diversity in the aboriginal diet. Oh fried bread, Indian tacos and corn soup are all fine, our soul food, so to speak, but I don't believe the Creator owns a deep fryer.

AMOS

May I?

SUMMER

Please.

AMOS takes one of the parfaits and gobbles it.

AMOS

I remember eating chokecherries as a kid. But Summer my love, you have done the impossible. You have improved on my memory. This is lovely. Good job. I'd double your per diem if I paid you any.

SUMMER

So you think I should continue? Making hybrid foods?

AMOS

If they come out this good, I think we can start a whole new food revolution. Chokecherry parfait ... I like it.

SUMMER

Oh goody. I'll start thinking up ideas immediately.

AMOS

Try and come up with something to do with salmon. We have lots of salmon.

SUMMER

Salmon. Got it. You're so good to me Amos. I love you.

AMOS

Of course you do. I'm an Elder. It comes with the beaded belt. Now get back to work.

SUMMER
Yes, we must hurry and finish our preparations for the dinner hour approaches. There will be many hungry Elders here, eager to fill their empty bellies.

AMOS
I couldn't have put it better myself. You check on the casserole and I'll start with the macaroni soup.

SUMMER
Hey, I have an idea! Macaroni and tofu soup! Nutritious and tasty. Think about it.

As she leaves, she raises her fist defiantly in the air in a radical pose.

SUMMER
Free Leonard Peltier!

AMOS
(*less enthusiastically*) Free Leonard Peltier.

SUMMER exits.

AMOS
I'm all for freeing Peltier but does she have to do that every time she leaves the room? Christ, the first time she did it I thought she was going to punch me.

PROF. SAVAGE enters the cafeteria. He spots AMOS working away and slowly approaches him. It's a few seconds before AMOS notices the scrutiny.

AMOS
Yes, can I help you?

SAVAGE
Yes. Are you married?

A suspicious AMOS puts a large dish between him and PROF. SAVAGE.

SAVAGE

Then again, perhaps your age prevents you from being part of the study. What are you, about 55, 60 maybe? Somewhat past the optimum survey age. However, it is supposed to be a cross-section of as broad a spectrum as possible, to get a true representation of the culture.

AMOS

Oh I get it. Okay, let's make this quick. I am Mohawk. I am from the Six Nations Reserve. I have partial command of my language. No, I am not diabetic. Yes, I have played snowsnakes in the past. No, I have never been an iron worker. Yes, I am Longhouse. No, I have never personally raised corn, beans and squash in my back yard. Yes, I am distantly related to E. Pauline Johnson, but not Joseph Brant. My mother was a clan mother and my father could sing every Hank Williams Sr. song ever written. That should about cover my humble Mohawk existence, Mr. Anthropologist. Now, if you don't mind, I have a Jesuit ... I mean turkey to roast.

SAVAGE

I'm sure that's all very interesting but frankly I'm more interested in your sex life.

AMOS

Son, if this is going where I think it's going, trust me, it ain't going. I got off the train at least two stops back, on my way to another town on a different rail line. You'll just have to wait for the next train. (*yelling*) Summer, could you come here for a second?

SAVAGE

Perhaps I should explain ...

AMOS

I think you've said enough.

SUMMER
You called, my Elder of love.

AMOS
This is my train station. Summer, could you please tell
this person that I am a happily attached man. Attached
to a woman. You. And that I used to box in my young
days and was quite good at it.

SAVAGE
No, I'm afraid you misunderstand me. I'm working on
a research paper dealing with the courtship rituals and
sexual habits of the contemporary aboriginal. I'm here
at this Elders' conference doing research.

SUMMER
Ooh, academia!! The eternal pursuit of knowledge. Do
you have a specific hypothesis you're exploring?

SAVAGE
Indeed I do. It is my belief that within the Native
community exists a hitherto unknown form of
socialization. I'm talking about a culture-specific
method of dating and courting. One that has evolved
gradually in the last one hundred years. We are all
familiar with the story of the warrior bringing a deer or
moose home to his beloved's father, proving his
prowess as a hunter. But in today's world, much has
changed. Less moose and deer. People now hunt for a
good video store. How does a Native man today woo
and court his intended? It is my belief that the
romantic Native has augmented the traditional with the
contemporary. The times, the culture, the people have
changed, and I want to document that change.

AMOS
But why concentrate on anthropological sex?

25

PROFESSOR
Indian pottery was booked solid. So, may I count on
your support?

AMOS
Well, I don't know ...

SUMMER
Oh come on Amos, don't you want to advance the
knowledge of your people?

AMOS
Well yes, but sex is a kind of private thing. I'm an old-
fashioned guy that way.

PROFESSOR
I assure you everything is confidential and private. No
one will get hurt.

AMOS
Said the white man to the Indian.

SAVAGE
I have a release form, a legally binding contract that
will guarantee it.

AMOS
Again, said the white man to the Indian.

SUMMER
Oh Amos, you must do it.

AMOS
I don't have to do anything. Being old has given me
the right to be fussy..

SUMMER
Please.

AMOS
Geez, Summer ... Okay.

SUMMER
Isn't he wonderful?

AMOS
The things I do for you.

PROFESSOR
Excellent. When can we set up an appointment?

AMOS
Maybe later, once all the cooking is done.

SUMMER
And if I may, Professor, I too would consent to an interview.

SAVAGE
I'm sorry but I must limit my interview subjects to those of aboriginal heritage.

SUMMER
But ...

PROFESSOR
Otherwise, it might taint the results.

SUMMER is silent.

AMOS
Professor, Summer does share some Native heritage.

PROFESSOR
She does? Oh, I'm sorry. I just assumed ...

AMOS
What she lacks in quantity, she more than makes up for in quality. I like to think of her as the bitters in my cocktail of life.

SUMMER
Ah, that's so sweet.

PROFESSOR
My error. I would be delighted to include you in our survey.

AMOS
Good. Excellent. Great. Now get out. We'll have plenty of time to talk after the feast.

PROFESSOR
I'll be in touch.

SAVAGE exits.

SUMMER
That was very nice of you to come to my rescue. You seem to rescue me a lot.

AMOS
Yeah I know. I'm your red knight in shining buckskin. Now cook!

SUMMER
I will cook you something extra special. Something fit for a warrior. How about cheese manicotti with cheese made from caribou milk?

AMOS
Sounds ... delicious.

SUMMER
And I think I know where to get some in this town! Isn't this exciting!

SUMMER jogs off happily into the kitchen.

AMOS
Ah Summer, you have so much to give. Why do you always have to give it to me?

Scene Four

THE WARRIOR WHO NEVER SLEEPS and MARTHA enter the cafeteria.

WARRIOR

And this is where the main feast shall be. Perhaps you are hungry now and I can get you something?

MARTHA

Young man, I've been meaning to ask you, is that a Mountie jacket you're wearing?

WARRIOR

You noticed. I wear it as a symbol to show our oppressors that I am not frightened of them. It is to show my contempt for my enemies and to demonstrate my bravery. It is my form of counting coup. I took it from a drycleaner's when he wasn't looking. It's part of what makes me the Warrior Who Never Sleeps.

MARTHA

Your mother must be so proud. Where is that Marianne when you need her?

WARRIOR

I can go search for her, if you wish.

MARTHA

No, better not. That woman would eat you alive, especially in the mood she's in. Word of advice young man, stay away from her if you value your sanity.

WARRIOR

But she is your daughter.

MARTHA

That she is. And I love her dearly but she needs elbow room.

WARRIOR
I will honour her elbow room. I am no threat to her.

MARTHA
Young man, you're young, cute, and look pretty good
in that uniform of yours. You're like a male Catholic
school girl. Marianne thinks she's ready to climb back
in the saddle again but I think she needs to walk a bit
first.

*AMOS comes racing out of the kitchen and disappears out
a nearby door.*

MARTHA
Who was that?

WARRIOR
I believe that was Amos. Another wise Elder to guide
us.

*AMOS comes racing through again, this time carrying a
fire extinguisher, disappearing back into the kitchen.*

MARTHA
I think your wise Elder may need some guidance of his
own.

*THE WARRIOR rushes into the kitchen, which now has
some smoke pouring out. A nervous MARTHA grabs a
glass of water on the table. She hears thumping, coughing,
and some crashes coming form the other room. Finally,
THE WARRIOR drags AMOS out the door. Still worried
about fire, MARTHA throws the water on both of them.
THE WARRIOR lays AMOS down on the ground.*

WARRIOR
I can save him.

*THE WARRIOR begins to give him mouth to mouth
resuscitation but AMOS throws him off.*

AMOS

It was just a small grease fire. I don't need mouth to mouth.

WARRIOR

I was just trying to help.

AMOS

Son, the last time a man kissed me was my father on my eighth birthday, but I thank you for the concern. Now help me up.

THE WARRIOR helps AMOS up.

MARTHA

You okay, Mister?

AMOS

Fine, a little annoyed with myself but I'll live.

WARRIOR

Amos, this is Martha Kakina, one of our Elders here to teach us the wonders of the Ojibway language.

AMOS

Hi, my name's Amos. I don't normally meet people under these conditions so I hope you'll forgive my unsightly appearance.

MARTHA

I've lived through a few grease fires of my own.

AMOS

Ojibway, huh? From where?

MARTHA

Otter Lake.

AMOS

Haven't been there in years. Beautiful place though. You're a language expert huh?

MARTHA
I wouldn't say expert. I just know my words.

AMOS
That sounds like an expert to me.

AMOS
Uh, Warrior Who Never Sleeps, what shall we do about all that smoke?

WARRIOR
I'm surprised the fire alarms haven't gone off.

AMOS
I disconnected them. I find they can be annoying in the heat of the moment. Some of my cooking methods are a little unusual.

WARRIOR
Wasn't there already a fire extinguisher in there?

AMOS
It's propping open the door.

WARRIOR
I will alert the custodian.

AMOS
The sooner, the better.

THE WARRIOR exits.

AMOS
Good boy that Warrior, got a good heart.

MARTHA
You know him?

AMOS
A little. My hearing isn't what it used to be. First time he told me his name, I thought he said he was "The Whore Who Never Sleeps." I thought: "At least he's

honest." He's just a little ambitious about his heritage. We all went through that phase.

MARTHA

When I was his age, a lot of us wanted to look white. My, how things have changed.

AMOS

I don't think you're allowed to collect your senior citizen's cheque until you have said, "My, how things have changed," a few dozen times. Would you like some tea?

MARTHA

At last. A civilized man. (*pause*) I hope you don't mean none of the funny-smelling tea youngsters like. I only drink black tea.

AMOS

And black tea you shall have. Mind if I join you? How do you want it?

AMOS pours two cups of tea.

MARTHA

Black please.

AMOS

No sugar? That's very un-Indian of you.

MARTHA

I used to be very Indian. Used to be a four tablespoon Indian woman up until a few years ago. Blood sugar was doing funny things. Doctor said no more sugar. Though every once in a while, I do slip myself some honey.

AMOS produces a jar of honey.

MARTHA

I shouldn't. Should I?

AMOS

I won't tell. And I know the number for 911.

MARTHA

If Marianne finds out, she'll kill me. Oh what the heck.
It's about time I caused her some grief. Give me a
teaspoon.

AMOS does just that. MARTHA smells the tea, then sips it.

MARTHA

You brew nice tea, Amos.

AMOS

It's easy with lovely company. (*toasting*) To many more
years of tea drinking.

They clink glasses and sip again.

MARTHA

You know, once, I tried to figure out how much tea I
had drank in my lifetime.

AMOS

How could you possibly do that?

MARTHA

Well, my mother told me that she started giving me
some tea just after I turned one. I figure I must have
had at least four cups of tea a day, for almost sixty
years. What do you think that would come out to?

AMOS does some figuring on a pad of paper.

AMOS

That comes out to ... I could be wrong but I think
that's about eighty-seven thousand, six hundred cups.
No, I'm wrong, that would be eighty-seven thousand,
six hundred and one cups. That's a hell of a lot of tea.

*MARTHA is sitting there, silent, giving AMOS a cold,
condemning look.*

AMOS
    What? Is something wrong?

MARTHA
    You said the "H" word.

AMOS
    The "H" ... Hell?

MARTHA
    You said it again. I will not sit here and listen to this
    kind of language, tea or no tea.

AMOS
    I didn't mean any disrespect. It just sort of slipped out.
    I respectfully apologize.

MARTHA
    I accept your apology. It's nice to share a cup of tea
    with a man with manners.

AMOS
    Thank you. And let me say, just looking at you makes
    me think they must be robbing the cradle looking for
    Elders for this here conference. You should be down
    competing at that Miss Indian World contest.

MARTHA
    Are you sure there's only tea in your cup? I'm surprised
    a man as polite and kitchen-oriented as you ain't been
    caught by a woman yet.

    AMOS is still fiddling with some calculations.

AMOS
    Well, I guess technically I have.

MARTHA
    You have a wife?

AMOS

Well, kinda, sort of. Maybe. Depends on how you define wife.

MARTHA

Married in the Church. In the presence of God. With a license.

AMOS

That's a pretty specific definition. Let's just say I'm severely going steady.

MARTHA

A man your age should be married.

AMOS

Was once. She passed on a few years back and well, the Creator saw fit to deliver unto me, in my golden years, a woman of unusual talents. Holy mackerel! Do you realize that in your lifetime, you have drank about twenty-one thousand, nine hundred litres of tea! That's a lot of tea! Jesus ...

> MARTHA *stiffens up but* AMOS *notices this. He immediately starts singing.*

AMOS

" ... loves the little children. All the children of the world." Don't you just love that hymn?

MARTHA

I take it you are not a Christian.

AMOS

Not the "in the Church, in the presence of God, with a license" kind. I was raised more traditionally but I think they all teach pretty much the same good message, only they use different textbooks.

MARTHA
Hmmmm.

SUMMER enters.

SUMMER
Amos! Amos! I can't believe I'm going to meet Miss
Indian World. We have definitely got to cook
something up special for her. I hear she's Tlingit from
Alaska and won her crown by shooting a caribou at
four hundred yards with a .303 rifle. In her honor, I
have come up with this new recipe for a western
sandwich made with turtle eggs, a lot lower in
cholesterol. Doesn't that sound yummy?

AMOS
Summer dear, the stove, you're cooking ...

SUMMER
I know, I know but I thought I should get busy locating
some turtle eggs immediately. I was fairly sure I could
find this turtle egg wholesaler just outside of Barrie. I
did turn the stove off though. I'd better fire it up
again.

*SUMMER exits into the kitchen. There is a pause. She exits
out of the kitchen.*

SUMMER
What happened to the kitchen?

AMOS
You turned the burners off. Not the oven.

SUMMER
Oh my God. I am so sorry. All the knobs look alike. I
always said gas stoves were bad for the environment.
You must be so angry at me.

AMOS
No. I'm not. Just be more careful next time.

SUMMER
Oh, I will. I promise. (*to MARTHA*) I just sometimes get
so excited about meeting all the interesting and
knowledgeable people at these wonderful functions.
Elders' conferences are perfect opportunities to grow
and enlighten myself as to the plethora of traditional
teachings available in this big, magnificent world, don't
you agree?

MARTHA tries to respond but with little opportunity.

SUMMER
And with Miss Indian World coming I mean really …
it's just almost too exciting but here I am going on and
on. You must forgive me and my ramblings, you're an
Elder, you can do that and I thank you but anyway, yes,
the caribou milk, I' ve located a couple quarts but I'm
not sure how long it takes to make the cheese but …

MARTHA
Who are you?

AMOS
Summer, this is Martha Kakina. She's here holding a
workshop on …

MARTHA
They tell me the Ojibway language.

SUMMER
Oh, I am being so rude. Sometimes my mouth runs
faster than a rabbit. Martha Kakina! Keeper of the
Annishnaabe language. What an honour. Aabiji
nmaamiikwendam gii-nkweshkoonaan. Aabji go
ngagwejtoon ji zhaayaan, ji-kinoomooyin

gdonbwaakaawin. (I am so proud to have met you. I will make it a point to attend and be taught your wisdom.)

MARTHA

Good Heavens! You speak Annishnaabe? But aren't you ...

SUMMER

Nwaabshkiiye? Zaagjeying eta. Aabji nii ngichinendam baangii anishinaabewyaan. (White? Only in appearance. For I am proud to say, one sixty-fourth Native.)

MARTHA

One sixty-fourth huh? I guess it takes all kinds.

SUMMER

And let me compliment you on retaining your language regardless of the zealous onslaught of cultural genocide sponsored by the various religious organizations.

MARTHA

I beg your pardon?

SUMMER

I thank the Creator that you and your command of the language weren't one of the people destroyed by governmental and Christian myopia.

AMOS

Uh Summer ...

SUMMER

You know, I have heard so many horror stories about the tragedies visited upon our Native people by the Church. You were lucky to escape the clutches of the Christian conversion machine.

MARTHA

(*coldly*) I see. You don't like the Church.

SUMMER

It's not that. It's just not very ... Native.

MARTHA

And you are?

SUMMER

You know what I mean.

MARTHA

Yes. I do.

SUMMER

Well, I better try and clean up my mess. If I don't,
Amos might just pick up his blanket and leave, as they
say.

> *SUMMER gives nervous AMOS a quick kiss.*

MARTHA

Are you his ...

SUMMER

Yep. I'm his buz'gem. Aren't I, honey?

AMOS

Buz'gem?

SUMMER

It's Ojibway for boyfriend or girlfriend.

MARTHA

(*to AMOS*) What did your first wife die of ? Her tricycle
fall over?

AMOS

I know we're an unusual couple but ...

MARTHA

It's okay. I'm not one to judge. You're a grown man. Grown men can do what they want. And justify it anyway they want. And they usually do.

SUMMER

I'm sorry. I don't understand.

MARTHA

That's because you're young, dear. What you may lack in understanding, you more than make up for in prettiness. An equitable trade for most men. Give it a few years.

AMOS

I don't think you're being fair.

MARTHA

Maybe not but only God can truly judge. Now if you'll excuse me, I'm off to find a grammar school. I need a date for the feast tonight.

SUMMER

Is it the fact that we are so far apart in age that upsets you?

MARTHA

The way I figure it, I still own my husband's eight-track player, but I'm smart enough to know that a CD don't belong in it. We have no control over who we are. But we have complete control over what we do. Thank you for the tea. Now if you'll excuse me, (*to SUMMER*) I'll be going now before a roving band of Baptists tries to drown me.

MARTHA exits.

SUMMER

Amos, what's her problem?

AMOS
　Nothing a good colonic wouldn't cure.

Scene Five

*An empty office. The door opens and PROFESSOR SAVAGE
enters, followed by MARIANNE.*

MARIANNE
Oh wow. That wasn't some line. You do actually have
an office.

She picks up a name plate on the desk.

MARIANNE
With your actual name. Cool. You must be a professor,
none of these books have been made into movies.

PROFESSOR
Make yourself comfortable.

MARIANNE
Should I be lying down on the couch?

PROFESSOR
I'm not a psychiatrist. I'm a cultural anthropologist.

MARIANNE
What's the difference?

PROFESSOR
About forty thousand a year. Now, Mrs. Kakina ...

MARIANNE
Miss. I'm recently divorced. Separated. Whatever you
want to call it. I'm now foot loose and fancy free. No
ropes hold me. I'm a wild spirit with no corral. You get
my drift, doctor?

SAVAGE
(*writing furiously*) Yes I do ... free agent, corral, and
ropes ... and please call me Professor. It's less formal.

MARIANNE
You're the doctor, Professor. So what can I do for you?

43

PROFESSOR

Now I've explained about the research I'm doing ...

MARIANNE

Admit it. That's just some excuse to talk dirty to me.

SAVAGE

Maybe you misunderstood ...

MARIANNE

Try not to use too many big words. I'm just an innocent little girl from the Rez.

PROFESSOR

I see. Perhaps we ...

MARIANNE

Native sexuality, huh? If you knew my ex-husband, you'd realize what a contradiction in terms that is.

PROFESSOR

Ms Kakina, can we please get on with this? I would really appreciate a more serious approach. Now, tell me about your sex life.

MARIANNE

Not without dinner and a movie first. Whatever happened to warming up to me with a few innocent questions? Some casual comments about my first kiss. What do you like to do on a date? Have you ever been arrested for disturbing the peace? Normal questions like that. It's all sex, sex, sex!

PROFESSOR

It's interesting that you said sex three times in an obviously agitated manner.

MARIANNE

Well, if you're lucky, sex should be done in an obviously agitated manner. Or do white people do it differently, professor?

PROFESSOR

Ahh! Finally a nugget of knowledge. I take it you've never been with a white man?

MARIANNE

I've thought about it but the only ones that ask me out all look like Gilligan.

PROFESSOR

Funny you should say that, I once did a research paper on the underlying sexual tensions apparent in the text and subtext of that show. The homo-erotic, submissive/dominant undercurrents evident in the Skipper/Gilligan relationship made for some fascinating interpretations. And you should have read my addendum concerning the Mary Ann and Ginger interaction, the archetypal innocent farm girl and Hollywood sex symbol on a romantic tropical island. My course director passed that paper around for months. I understand it's still the most signed out paper in the university library.

MARIANNE

You academics sure are a wild bunch. I don't know if you noticed but my name is Marianne too. (*singing*) The professor and Marianne ...

PROFESSOR

What a coincidence. Ms Kakina ...

MARIANNE

Marianne.

PROFESSOR
Marianne then. We're here to talk about you.

MARIANNE
My sex life. What's left of it.

PROFESSOR
As part of a larger picture.

MARIANNE
There is no larger picture, Professor. I wish there was.

PROFESSOR
You are a very unusual woman, Marianne.

MARIANNE
A sentence like that can either be a compliment or a criticism.

PROFESSOR
In my work, it's often unwise to compliment your subjects.

MARIANNE
Your lab rats will get jealous? Tell you what, I'll tell you something private and intimate about myself, and then you tell me something private and intimate about yourself.

PROFESSOR
Bartering is not usually allowed during interviews. Besides, my personal history is irrelevant to this project.

MARIANNE
Didn't your parents ever teach you to share? You don't get any cookies without any milk.

PROFESSOR
This is very irregular.

MARIANNE
Take a laxative. Do we have a deal?

The PROFESSOR is silent, then nods.

MARIANNE
Good. So, when did you lose your virginity?

Scene Six

THE WARRIOR WHO NEVER SLEEPS is smudging the commons room and mumbling a prayer under his breath. The fire alarm goes off. He quickly grabs a chair, climbs on top of it, and struggles to turn it off, finally succeeding. He is unaware that the burning sweetgrass is directly under a sprinkler system until he turns and notices it. He quickly brushes the smoke away. Making sure everything is okay, he gets down from the chair.

MARIANNE runs in.

MARIANNE

Hey , Warrior Who Never Looks Before He Leaps, what's all the noise? .

WARRIOR

No! My name is the Warrior Who Never Sleeps! Sleeps!

MARIANNE

Oh, excuse me, Warrior Who Never Sleeps. I thought I heard an alarm or something.

WARRIOR

I was ... testing the alarms to make sure they worked properly.

MARIANNE

That was a sweetgrass alarm, wasn't it? Those things can be real sensitive. So, is this where Miss Indian World is going to do her thing?

WARRIOR

That is why I must cleanse it for her. I alone carry that responsibility.

MARIANNE

I bet your heart's going pitter patter at the thought of meeting her.

WARRIOR
What do you mean?

MARIANNE
You strike me as a single guy. Or am I wrong? Is there a little Miss Warrioress Who Keeps You Up All Night somewhere back home?

WARRIOR
No. I walk my path alone.

MARIANNE
Well who knows? Maybe you'll get lucky with little Miss Indian World. I hear these show business people love dark sunglasses.

WARRIOR
My journey is long and I must walk it alone. It is my way.

MARIANNE
Me too. Now. Ever been married, or something similar?

WARRIOR
No.

MARIANNE
I was. For over ten years. Nice Guy. David. Sure wish he looked like that statue David they have over in Italy. Instead of marble he was made of Kraft Dinner. Oh well, all water under the bridge. I'm probably boring you with all this.

WARRIOR
Oh ... not at all. I love hearing divorce stories. Really I do, but I must continue on my mission.

MARIANNE
Oh yes. Miss Indian World and the smudged room. I wonder what she's like?

WARRIOR

I have not had the opportunity to meet her but I have it on good authority that she has great patience. Part of her talent competition was making a basket from scratch. She's Pomo and I heard it took six hours for her to finish the basket and the judges had to sit and watch her through the whole thing.

MARIANNE

Wow. Six hours of basket weaving. I wonder how long it takes her to make Tupperware?

THE WARRIOR checks his watch.

WARRIOR

I am late. I must go to a helper's meeting before the conference begins. But the room isn't finished being cleansed.

MARIANNE

Oh probably my fault with all my gabbing. Do you want me to finish it for you?

WARRIOR

You know how to use sweetgrass?

MARIANNE

Do campers shit in the woods? Go to your meeting. The room's almost done anyways.

WARRIOR

I thank you.

MARIANNE

And thank you for listening.

WARRIOR

Sometimes that is the best thing a warrior can do. A warrior of silence. I know what it's like to be alone. My heart cries with you.

MARIANNE
You? I thought nothing touched you that wasn't
wearing a dreamcatcher.

WARRIOR
My journey to becoming the Warrior Who Never Sleeps
was not easy. There were moments when I almost lost
sight and gave in to personal demons.

MARIANNE
You had demons?

WARRIOR
All I can tell you is stay strong. The rapids are
dangerous but eventually you will come upon calm
waters and your path will once again be in the sunlight.
I must go now.

MARIANNE
Wow, maybe there's actually something behind those
shades.

THE WARRIOR raises his fist in a protest sign.

WARRIOR
Oka forever!

He exits.

MARIANNE
Oka ... doky.

*MARIANNE takes off her jacket, tossing to a distant chair,
and then continues with the sweetgrass cleansing, which
takes a few seconds.*

MARIANNE
There, that should keep all the bad spirits out and all
the good spirits in. Psychic storm windows.

MARIANNE walks to the door to exit but is prevented by AMOS and SUMMER entering, carrying trays of assorted munchies. SUMMER is somewhat upset.

SUMMER

Don't make excuses. I don't think she liked me. Why? I have a good spirit and a noble cause. It's because I have some white blood isn't it? Isn't it!

AMOS

Summer, you don't have "some" white blood. You're sixty-three sixty-fourths white. That's pretty white. That's damn near albino for Christ sakes.

SUMMER

Amos, what are you trying to say?

AMOS

Well .... .

They both then notice MARIANNE standing there. They stop.

MARIANNE

Don't mind me. Please continue.

AMOS

If you'll excuse us ... Hey, you look familiar. I know you.

MARIANNE

I was thinking that too. Amos right? Yeah, we used to bump into each other at the Pow wows a couple years back. You're looking pretty good. Lost some weight I see. What's your secret?

AMOS

I have a twenty-five-year-old girlfriend.

MARIANNE
Beats the hell out of a Stairmaster I guess. And would this be your personal trainer?

AMOS
Summer, this is … I'm sorry …

MARIANNE
Marianne.

SUMMER
Do you dislike me?

MARIANNE
Can I get to know you first?

AMOS
Summer, you're taking this all out of proportion.

SUMMER
(*to MARIANNE*) Do I look white to you?

MARIANNE
Is this a trick question?

SUMMER
Do you resent me for the way I look? Even though I too am a member of the great aboriginal nation?

MARIANNE
Which nation? The Cleveland Indians?

SUMMER
See! Even she makes fun of me. I try and I try but it's wasted.

AMOS
There was this older lady who …

SUMMER
… was very rude to me and I want to know why.

AMOS
    I think she was a little thrown off by the difference in
    our ages, not so much your skin colour.
SUMMER
    I could read the subtext. I always see it in the eyes of
    Native women. They resent me because I am with you
    and am the colour of winter, not summer, and that is
    not fair. I should not be judged until I am understood.
MARIANNE
    Don't worry about it. Every culture has its jerks. She
    was probably just some crazy old lady who had the hots
    for Amos herself. If you want, I'll punch her out for
    you.
SUMMER
    Amos, am I being silly?
AMOS
    Not any more than normal. Now, can we finish setting
    up for the social? The munchies won't make it in here
    all by themselves.
MARIANNE
    (*sniffing*) Food!? You have food? What do you got?

    SUMMER puts a tray down and offers MARIANNE a
    nibble of food. MARIANNE takes it.
SUMMER
    Now this is brand new. I created it this afternoon.
    Please be honest with me and tell me what you think.
MARIANNE
    What do you call it?
SUMMER
    Chocolate moose.

MARIANNE

(*chewing*) Hmm, sweet and kind of chewy.

SUMMER

Do you like it?

MARIANNE

Takes some getting used to but ... kind of sticks to your ribs.

SUMMER

Actually, it is a rib.

MARIANNE

That explains the crunchiness.

SUMMER

Please, take another. She likes it, Amos!

MARIANNE

It's almost like it's chewing back.

SUMMER

You have just made my day, my aboriginal sister. I offer you a heart-filled thanks.

MARIANNE

(*still chewing*) Doesn't seem to want to go down. It's almost like it's fighting me.

AMOS

Why don't you go back to the kitchen and get the cold cuts?

SUMMER

Okay but what if I run into that woman again?

MARIANNE

Tell her you know somebody who'll thump her out. I'll get my mother to do it. Their elderness will cancel each other out.

SUMMER

That won't be necessary but thank you anyway. It's nice to see a supportive face in my journey.

SUMMER exits.

AMOS

That was very nice of you to bolster her self-confidence.

MARIANNE

Hey, we're all part of the sisterhood. Hey, you know, I've been chewing on this chocolate moose for a few minutes now and ... I think this thing has gotten bigger.

AMOS

Summer's cooking is rather unusual.

MARIANNE

I hope you don't mind me saying this but you two make an ... um ...

AMOS

Unusual couple?

MARIANNE

You two married?

AMOS

Summer thinks marriage is ... how does she put it ... "an archaic device perpetrated by a class-based society for the specific purpose of objectifying by leasing the female gender to men with the sole purpose of rendering them chattel."

MARIANNE

Interesting. Any idea what it means?

AMOS

I don't think she wants to get married.

MARIANNE
And you do?

AMOS
I don't know what I want. Or if I want anything at all.

MARIANNE
You're an Elder. You're supposed to know exactly what you want.

AMOS shrugs and exits.

Scene Seven

*The PROFESSOR is interviewing THE WARRIOR WHO
NEVER SLEEPS, in his office. THE WARRIOR is handing
the PROFESSOR a form he has filled out.*

PROFESSOR

You're sure that's the name you want me to file you
under?

WARRIOR

That is what I am. That is who I am. I have spoken.

PROFESSOR

Okay, Mr. ... Sleeps, I'm going to be asking you a series
of questions concerning the dating and courtship rituals of your nation and generation. I would appreciate it
if you would answer them as honestly and accurately as
possible. Do you understand?

WARRIOR

Honesty is my code.

SAVAGE

I will put that down as a yes. Let's begin. How old are
you?

WARRIOR

That is an evil question. For age is an artificial
construct created by white society to theoretically
designate a person's worth. I do not subscribe to
manufactured classifications. The circle of life and
existence is eternal. My people only knew the age of
when you were born, when you became a man or
woman, and when you became an Elder. All other age
specifications are unnecessary.

SAVAGE

Okay. What is your address?

WARRIOR
That is a misleading question. I live where the sun
shines. Where the rain falls. Where the wind blows. I
am there. Where the aboriginal voice cries out for
vengeance ... where Native people gather for
ceremonies ... where the drum beats, that is my home.

SAVAGE
Colourful, yet annoying. Let's try something else. How
about ... What is your profession?

WARRIOR
That is an intelligent question. I am the conscience of
my people. I am the memory of our ancestors. I am the
spirit of our ways. I draw strength from our survival and
sustenance from our beliefs. My aboriginalism is my
survival, and my heritage is my pay cheque.

SAVAGE
Look ... Mr. Sleeps, this is getting us nowhere. I need
some concrete answers if this survey is to be accurate.
Are you capable of giving me coherent, honest
responses, free of hyperbole?

WARRIOR
On my ancestors' sacred memory, everything I tell you
is the truth.

SAVAGE
I don't want truth. I want information. Is that clear?

WARRIOR
I thought that was information. Wasn't it? Weren't you
informed?

PROFESSOR
Okay, maybe this is my fault. Perhaps we should narrow
our focus, try a different tack. Have you ever been in
love?

WARRIOR
That is a good question. To be Native is to understand the truest form of love. It is a love of the land, of the people, of a way of thinking. My upbringing has given me a secret insight into what you call love. To be Native is to love.

The amazed PROFESSOR stares at THE WARRIOR.

PROFESSOR
Yeah ... Mr. Sleeps, what is the value of the mathematical equation known as pi?

WARRIOR
Our ancient legends, preserved on birch bark, instruct us about the sacred circle of life, and within that circle, you have a radius ... aboriginal algebra, one of our lesser known teachings ...

The PROFESSOR lets his head fall with a mighty thump, to the desk in defeat.

PROFESSOR
Oh God, stop. Please make him stop.

Scene Eight

Back in the commons room, MARIANNE is sleeping on one of the couches. She tosses and turns a few times.

MARIANNE

(*moaning*) David ... David ... You're a peckerhead, David ... yeah, you ...

SUMMER enters, carrying a tray of pink drinks. She spots MARIANNE and puts the tray down. MARIANNE continues to mumble under her breath, when MARTHA and THE WARRIOR enter. SUMMER hides. MARTHA and THE WARRIOR hear MARIANNE and approach the sleeping, mumbling woman.

WARRIOR

What is she saying?

MARTHA

It's Ojibway.

MARIANNE

Enh, edetewshtigwed gdaaw. (Yep, you're a peckerhead)

MARTHA

Somebody is ... peckerhead.

MARIANNE wakes up with a start.

MARIANNE

Okay, I'm awake.

MARTHA

You should close your mouth when you sleep. And when you're awake sometimes too.

MARIANNE

What are you two doing here?

WARRIOR

I am showing your mother where she is holding her
workshop.

MARTHA

What's a workshop?

MARIANNE

Mom, it's where you will talk about speaking Ojibway
and I guess how it differs from English. That's what
you're getting paid the big bucks for.

MARTHA

But I've never done this before. I don't know how to
start.

MARIANNE

Well, what do you think the biggest difference between
the two languages is?

MARTHA

After a long day of speaking English, I sometimes feel
like taking my poor tired tongue out of my mouth and
putting it on a nice cool plate.

MARIANNE

Not the most academic of observations but I think it
says a lot, in a very Martha-type way. People love stuff
like that, that homespun stuff, don't they, The Warrior
Who Likes Sheep?

WARRIOR

Sleep! Sleep!

MARIANNE

Sleep. Sorry.

MARTHA

Marianne, I don't like the way this room is set up. I
think they have me standing against that bright

window. Nobody will see me if I stand there. Can you move the furniture for me?

WARRIOR

That is my responsibility. I will …

MARTHA

I was hoping you would take me to the cafeteria. I haven't had my lunch yet. Marianne's a big girl. She's not afraid of a few couches, are you Marianne?

MARIANNE

But it's his job …

MARTHA

Shh. Don't bother this young man. (*she puts her arm through his*) He's taking me to lunch. So, are you going to the feast tonight, my young and handsome helper? How old are you anyways?

MARIANNE

But Mom …

MARTHA

Shh, Mommy's busy. (*to WARRIOR*) You look very dashing in red.

They exit.

MARIANNE

Mom?

No response.

MARIANNE

Oh man! This is what husbands are for.

She moves the first couch and discovers SUMMER hiding behind it. They scare each other.

MARIANNE

What the hell are you doing behind there!

SUMMER
Is she gone?

MARIANNE
Who?

SUMMER
That horrible woman!

MARIANNE
What horrible woman? Are you talking about my
mother? Hey, you can't call my mother horrible. Only I
can do that. What's your problem lady?

SUMMER
She's the one I told you about. The one that was so
rude to me. Oh, I don't know what to do. I want to be
respectful of her years, and not aggravate the situation
but I too am an individual with feelings. My aboriginal
heart cries out for understanding.

MARIANNE
The one/sixty-fourth part of your aboriginal heart?

SUMMER
Yes. I know she has the right to her opinion, just as I
have the right to love Amos. Why must those come into
conflict? It is not our way.

MARIANNE
My mom's way is my mom's way. She can be stubborn
at times. Boy can she be stubborn. She's also quite old-
fashioned. It's probably the age difference. How far
apart are you and Amos?

SUMMER
Only thirty-five years!

MARIANNE
Ouch. That's not a May-December romance, that's a
couple months into the next calender.

SUMMER
I just appreciate the wisdom and gentleness of an older
man. Is that not a part of our culture?

MARIANNE
Tell me, why are you so proud of those few strands of
Native DNA? I mean, you are who you are but really,
one/sixty-fourth? That's an awful lot of Caucasian
genes to ignore. What's your last name?

SUMMER
Ducharme.

MARIANNE
You're French? With a name like Summer?

SUMMER
My real name is actually Agnes. And I am ... actually
French, except of course for the one ...

MARIANNE
... sixty-fourth part. Yes, I kinda figured. Agnes
Ducharme, huh? And what's wrong with being French?
Hey, I listen to Celine Dion, I root for the Montreal
Canadiens, French toast—I love it.

SUMMER
You think I should try to be more French?

MARIANNE
That's the key word right there. Try. Don't try to be
French. If you are, then you are. I think that's the
thing my mother sensed in you. That maybe you are
trying to be Native. Maybe trying a little too hard.

SUMMER

I hate people like that.

MARIANNE

How many of those necklaces, bracelets and rings do
you think it takes to be officially classified as a Native
person?

SUMMER

Too much?

MARIANNE

Not if you're in a Broadway musical.

SUMMER is silent for a moment.

MARIANNE

So what is it about Indians that you find so interesting?

SUMMER is silent.

MARIANNE

Can't be our fashion sense. There's only so many ways
you can wear denim.

SUMMER

It's your sense of belonging. You know who you are,
where you come from. After five hundred years of
surviving, you have a culture and a language. And a
pride. I respect that.

MARIANNE

Did you say … "you … have a culture … "?

Pause.

SUMMER

I said "you," didn't I? What should I do? Break up with
Amos? Trade in my Thunderbird for a Miatta? For so
long I have struggled to fit in, be a part of the circle.

MARIANNE

Boy, you really take this stuff seriously, don't you? Just remember ... You're still you.

SUMMER

But what does that mean?

MARIANNE

It means ... you be you.

SUMMER begins to think.

MARIANNE

Cool. You know, I think I'm beginning to get this Elder thing down ... And by the way, I'm still digesting that chocolate moose thing you gave me while back. It sure stays with you.

SUMMER

Here, try this. This might help.

She hands MARIANNE a pink drink from the tray.

MARIANNE

(*while taking a drink*) What is it?

SUMMER

It's a Salmon Shake.

MARIANNE spits it up.

SUMMER

Something wrong? Not enough salmon?

MARIANNE

No, it's fine. I had some for breakfast. I'll just nurse this a bit longer. I ... I have to go to the bathroom now. You go off and find yourself.

SUMMER

I must be myself. I must accept myself. I must become myself.

She takes off a necklace as she exits. A few seconds later,
MARIANNE's voice can be heard coming from the
bathroom.

MARIANNE
I think the meaning of life has something to do with
making sure there's a second roll of toilet paper in the
bathroom. (*pause*) Hello? Hello?

Scene Nine

*THE WARRIOR and MARTHA enter the cafeteria. THE
WARRIOR is clearly uncomfortable but MARTHA is
having fun, playing with his mind.*

WARRIOR

Perhaps I can get you a sandwich or something?

MARTHA

Perhaps you can.

WARRIOR

(*Yelling*) Amos! Amos!

MARTHA

Do you know I was married for twenty-nine years?

WARRIOR

That is very admirable. Two people that walk the path
together for so long must be very much in love.

MARTHA

He died eleven years ago. I'm very much alone.

WARRIOR

I promised you a sandwich. Amos! I need a sandwich.

THE WARRIOR spots food on a nearby table.

WARRIOR

How about a bagel? It's not bannock but it'll do in a
pinch. Would you like it toasted?

MARTHA

Yes please. I like it dark and toasty. Almost burnt.

WARRIOR

The bagel, right?

MARTHA

Of course.

AMOS enters.

AMOS

What's all the yelling about?

MARTHA

Hmmm, I'm trying to find out if the grass is greener on the other side of the fence.

AMOS

Hey boy, are you green grass?

WARRIOR

I am many things. The Creator has ...

AMOS

Oh just quit it. Just once I'd like to get a straight answer out of you. (*to MARTHA*) And you, I don't like you harassing Summer. She's insecure enough as it is.

MARTHA

I have not been harassing anybody. I'm entitled to my opinion and you're entitled to yours. Where is your buz'gem right now? Is it nap time?

AMOS

Actually she went to brush her teeth. Summer still has all of hers.

WARRIOR

I think I hear the Creator calling. I'd better be ...

MARTHA

Young man, what do you think of an old man who dates young women? Children practically?

WARRIOR

What do I think? I don't really believe it's my place to ...

MARTHA

See! He agrees with me. Dirty old man.

AMOS
Hey, did you hear what she called me? Did she call me
a dirty old man?

WARRIOR
I really wasn't ... I mean ...

MARTHA
If the moccasin fits ...

WARRIOR
Perhaps this is not the time ...

MARTHA
At least this young man here knows who he is. Unlike
some people around here who should know better.
He's got enough pride to know better than to do silly
things no self-respecting person would do.

WARRIOR
Why? What do you know?

AMOS
Look lady, you've obviously got some problems. I was
always taught to respect all kinds of people but every
once in a while ... you run into an Ojibway.

MARTHA
You're not Ojibway?

AMOS
I'm not short enough. Kanienkaha. Mohawk. Six
Nations.

MARTHA
Mohawk! You're Mohawk! Young man, want to hear a
story my parents used to tell me when I was just a
young girl?

WARRIOR
I really have to ...

MARTHA

A long, long time ago when I was a child, my mother would always tell me to be a good little girl or else the evil Nodweg would come into our village and take us away. All the people from my generation were told to behave because the Nodweg would get you.

WARRIOR

Ah ... what is a Nodweg?

MARTHA

A Mohawk.

WARRIOR

Oh boy.

MARTHA

It seems they are still stealing little girls. There's some truth in them old legends, huh?

AMOS

I did not steal Summer. She came to me for guidance ...

MARTHA

Guidance. Oh ... is that what Nodwegs call it.

AMOS

Warrior Who Never Sleeps, are you Ojibway or Mohawk?

WARRIOR

I'm Cree.

AMOS and MARTHA immediately dismiss him and his Creeness with a wave of their hands.

AMOS

Lady, this Nodweg has had enough. For your information, I have never stolen any children, let alone any Ojibway ones, though that wouldn't be remarkably

72

difficult since their mothers are always somewhere
playing bingo!

MARTHA

(*coldly*) You leave bingo alone.

AMOS

Or what? You'll wrap me in birchbark and pelt me with
wild rice?

MARTHA

Well, I think I better leave before somebody blockades
the doorway.

MARTHA exits.

AMOS

Word of advice, Warrior, stay away from Ojibway
women. They may look good but they seem to think it
either Ojibway or the highway.

*AMOS turns and exits, leaving behind the bewildered
WARRIOR, alone on stage. The toaster pops up the bagel.
He takes the bagel, butters it, and takes a bite.*

WARRIOR

What's wrong with being Cree?

Lights down.

End of Act One.

ACT TWO

Scene One

MARTHA is sitting in a chair in DR. SAVAGE's office.

MARTHA

Really mister, I don't have time for all this foolishness.
I've got things to attend to. Important things.

SAVAGE

I understand. This won't take long. You've heard about
the survey I'm doing?

MARTHA

Yes, Marianne told me about it. You remember her?

SAVAGE

Yes I do. A very interesting woman.

MARTHA

That's what the police used to say. Look, I was married
for twenty-nine happy years and had two healthy
children. That's as personal as I'm gonna get with you.
May I go now?

SAVAGE

Please, Mrs. Kakina, this is a very important research
project. Surely you can spare a few minutes?

MARTHA

Oh very well. But watch your manners. I don't tolerate
any dirty talk.

SAVAGE

Excellent. Now, Mrs. Kakina, how old were you when you were married?

MARTHA

Twenty-one years old. This is a comfy chair. Where can I get me one of these?

SAVAGE

It came with the office. Now how long did you date your husband before you got married?

MARTHA

Real leather. Bet it cost a fortune. Always wanted me a chair like this but couldn't really afford it. I keep hinting to Marianne but that girl can't take a hint no matter what. Her father was the same way. The contractions were five minutes apart before he bothered to wake up.

SAVAGE

Mrs. Kakina, how long did you and your husband date?

MARTHA

About a year. Things were different back then. None of this long term engagement stuff. Soon as the man figured you'd laugh at his jokes or the the woman found out if he snored or not, that was basically that. My son-in-law used to dress like you, Marianne's David. Too bad they got separated. I guess Marianne was too much a free spirit.

SAVAGE

If we could stay on topic here, Mrs. Kakina …

MARTHA

You a married man, Professor?

SAVAGE

Uh no.

MARTHA
Why not?

SAVAGE
I'm here to ask questions about you.

MARTHA
You got something wrong with you? You snore or something?

SAVAGE
Mrs. Kakina, try to focus. Now, since your husband passed away, have you been romantically involved with anybody?

MARTHA
Don't be silly. I got better things to do with my time than chase men all over the place. I wouldn't even know how. Why? You interested?

SAVAGE
Please, Mrs. Kakina. Let's keep this on a professional level.

MARTHA
I see one of your books is about the Iroquois. Mohawks are one of them, aren't they?

SAVAGE
Yes they are. Keepers of the Eastern Door I believe.

MARTHA
They're a strange bunch, aren't they? The Mohawks I mean.

SAVAGE
I'm really not at liberty to comment on that but ...

MARTHA
They have that, what do they call it ... matriarchal thing they're so proud of. But show me an Ojibway

home that's not run by a woman and I'll show you a single father.

SAVAGE

My research shows that they are quite adept at courting. They have many rituals geared towards pairing up.

MARTHA

You don't say! Like what?

SAVAGE

The Alligator Dance for example. The men get up to dance first. When a woman spots a gentleman she is interested in, she joins him on the dance floor. I should also point out that it's an insult for the man to refuse her participation.

MARTHA

The Alligator Dance huh? I didn't realize they had alligators in the Grand River. Goodness, and I thought our bloodsuckers were bad. How do you know all this?

SAVAGE

Occasionally my research requires me to attend various social functions. I have learned Mohawk women can be quite aggressive, when they want. However, once I start a discussion examining the socio-dynamic implications of trans-cultural objectivity in the face of New World economics, they eventually leave me alone.

MARTHA

You spend a lot of time by yourself, don't you Professor?

SAVAGE

I have a cat.

MARTHA
You might want to consider getting a second one. Oh well, I must be going.

SAVAGE
Please, Mrs. Kakina, I have so many questions to ask you.

MARTHA
Sonny, tell you what, you come to this social tonight and maybe once the food's done, we might have a chance to talk again. Besides, that Miss Indian World girl is supposed to show up. I hear she's cute.

SAVAGE
Miss Indian World? Isn't that the Pequot lady from the Foxwoods Casino who played blackjack for her traditional talent and won $24,000?

MARTHA
Could be. Good-bye, Professor. Say hello to your cat for me.

MARTHA exits. The PROFESSOR yells after her.

SAVAGE
His name is Beowulf ...

Scene Two

The commons room. THE WARRIOR WHO NEVER SLEEPS
is standing silent and alone, looking out a window.
MARIANNE enters, quickly grabbing the jacket she left
there earlier.

MARIANNE

Hey, Warrior Who Who's Not Very Deep, forgot my
jacket. So when's ...

No response. She looks out the window too.

MARIANNE

What's so interesting out there? It's a parking lot. It's a
nice parking lot but it's still a parking lot. What's so
fascinating?

WARRIOR

I am assessing my place in the universe.

MARIANNE

Assessing your place in the universe?

WARRIOR

Yes.

MARIANNE

Any particular reason?

WARRIOR

Yes.

More silence.

MARIANNE

Care to share it?

WARRIOR

No.

More silence.

MARIANNE

(*pointing*) Look, two people are doing it in that van.
Made you look! You got some problems those glasses
can't dim?

WARRIOR

It is my battle. Not yours.

MARIANNE

True. I don't know you but you're going to be looking
after my mother, so I want to be sure your bingo card
has all its numbers.

WARRIOR

It's hard being me.

MARIANNE

It's hard being you. How is it hard being you?

WARRIOR

Your mother spoke true words to me a little while ago.
They still are with me.

MARIANNE

What did she say this time?

WARRIOR

It's not what she said, it's what she made me see.
People don't respect who I am or what I stand for. I am
not taken seriously.

MARIANNE

For instance, by people like me?

Again THE WARRIOR is silent.

MARIANNE

I respect people for who they are. Sure I do. But is that
who you are? I don't know if it's female intuition, or
simply a hunch, but I think there's more to you than a

smart coat and sunglasses. At least I hope so because that's not a lot to hang your life on.

WARRIOR

But I am the Warrior Who Never ...

MARIANNE

... Sleeps. Yeah I know. It's on your name tag. But I have no idea what that name means.

MARTHA enters the room.

MARTHA

There you are. I was wondering where you took off to. Did you ask him?

MARIANNE

Haven't gotten the chance. We got into talking about assessing our places in the universe.

MARTHA

Oh, that's nice. You come to any answers?

MARIANNE

Just that people pick on him.

MARTHA

A good-looking, smart boy like him! No!

MARIANNE

Surprise, surprise.

MARTHA

Well, let's see what we can do about that. Young man, take off your glasses.

WARRIOR

I ... I can't. It's part of my warriorness.

MARTHA

You listen to me. I'm an Elder. Take those glasses off or I'll kick you in the ass till they fly off your head.

MARIANNE
She'll do it too.

WARRIOR
But you don't understand …

MARTHA
Look, my foot is leaving the ground …

MARIANNE
I'd be taking those glasses off right about now or
starting to run. I've seen the damage that foot can do.

*THE WARRIOR quickly removes his glasses, squinting at
the bright lights.*

MARTHA
There. That wasn't so hard, was it?

MARIANNE
You're right, Mom. He is kind of cute.

WARRIOR
Why did you make me take off my glasses?

MARTHA
Because in order to assess your place in the universe,
you gotta be able to see clearly. Something tells me you
were using those things to hide behind.

MARIANNE
What about the Mountie jacket, Mom?

WARRIOR
Not my Mountie jacket. I like my Mountie jacket.

MARTHA
Let the boy keep his Mountie jacket. A man's got to
have a few toys to play with. Tell me young man, were
you always like this?

WARRIOR
Like what?

MARTHA
Being soooo Indian, it's gotta hurt. Be honest. I'm an old lady and I don't want the last thing I may hear on this Earth to be lies coming from a man in a Mountie jacket.

MARIANNE
It's an easy enough question. Were you human once?

WARRIOR
A long time ago, in a Reserve far, far away, I was once like you. That was in ... the before time.

MARIANNE
I take it this was back in the time you were known as the Warrior Who Could Sleep. What were you like, in the before time?

WARRIOR
I was a ...

MARIANNE
A what?

WARRIOR
A ... a ... geek.

MARTHA
He doesn't look Greek.

MARIANNE
No Mom, I think he said geek. You did say geek, right?

WARRIOR
Yes. I was the guy nobody wanted to know. The guy nobody noticed. That guy that ...

MARIANNE
... was in the audio/visual club in school?

WARRIOR
No. The library club.

MARIANNE
Ouch. Geek alert.

WARRIOR
I didn't like myself. I was tired of being a nobody. The butt of jokes. A geek.

MARIANNE
Oh come on, every kid thinks they're a geek at some time. It's part of being a kid.

WARRIOR
Then you tell me. It came to me one night as I worked away in my room, compiling the world's first Klingon/Cree dictionary.

MARIANNE
I think you should get some bonus marks for geek creativity.

WARRIOR
I was up to the "g"s when I found myself momentarily stumped over the translation of "grandmother." The Klingons have a slightly different perception of family relations and I went to my father for help. I can still remember it. He was sitting in his chair, watching the hockey game. I explained my dilemma and waited for a response. Without saying a word he just stared at me. It was all there in his eyes. It was then I knew I had crossed over the line from fan, to nerd, to full-fledged geekdom. I was a Native geek ... a neek. There had to be a change.

MARTHA
You found God?

WARRIOR
No. I stopped watching cable. I made a solemn vow to transform. I decided to dedicate my life to something

important. To something not spawned by a thirty-five-year-old television series. To become somebody people would notice, respect, and remember. That was the day I became the Warrior Who Never Sleeps.

There is a solemn silence.

MARIANNE
A Klingon/Cree dictionary?! That's the stupidest thing I've ever heard!

MARTHA
Marianne ...

MARIANNE
That's the most unusual thing I have ever encountered.

MARTHA
So why are you doing this "reassessing your life" thing?

WARRIOR
Something you said to Amos.

MARIANNE
What did you say to Amos?

MARTHA
None of your business. Other than he's a Nodweg.

MARIANNE
Oh for Pete's sakes, mother. You're a grown woman. Mohawks are not bogeymen! They're ... Mohawks. And what's this got to do with the Warrior Who Likes Pleats.

MARTHA
Don't ask me. I'm just here to talk Ojibway.

MARIANNE
What do Klingons, your father, my mother, and a Mohawk cook have to do with you reassessing your life?

WARRIOR

I'm not sure being The Warrior Who Never Sleeps is
the path I want to follow. It takes an awful lot of
concentration to be this way. And an awful lot of
reading. Keeping up with all the Native-oriented
political and social issues is mind-boggling. I've lost
track of how many protests I've been to, and how many
vigils I've kept. When I'm out at night, these glasses
have made me run into so many trees and ditches, I
have to get this thing drycleaned at least three times a
week.

MARTHA

Maybe you're not this Warrior boy. Maybe you're just
somebody who is confused. Marianne used to be
confused about who she was. She used to tell me,
"Mom, there's a young, beautiful, thin, woman
struggling to get out of me." I told her, "Nope. You are
who you are."

MARIANNE

Thanks Mom.

WARRIOR

Then who am I?

MARTHA

Marianne, who is he?

MARIANNE

Sure, save the hard questions for me. What's your real
name?

WARRIOR

My real name? It's the Warrior Who N ...

MARIANNE

Wrong answer. What is your real, real, real name? The name your mother and father called you while they were potty training you. That name.

Beat.

WARRIOR

Ted.

MARIANNE

Ted? Did you say Ted?

WARRIOR

Ted Cardinal.

MARTHA

(*indicating his jacket*) Makes sense, cardinals are red.

MARIANNE

Well, Ted Cardinal. It's a pleasure to meet you. I'm Marianne and this is my mother Martha Kakina.

MARTHA

. My brother's name was Ted. It's a good name. Be proud of it.

WARRIOR

I just don't feel like a Ted anymore.

MARIANNE

C'mon, find your inner Tedness. It was there before. What's your name? C'mon, tell us again?

WARRIOR

Ted. My name is Ted Cardinal.

MARTHA

Ted, sometimes it's good to be somebody you want to be. But it's always a good idea to be who you are.

MARIANNE

You read that somewhere.

MARTHA
I did not. My mother used to say that all the time.

MARIANNE
Grandma never said more than ten words in the eighteen years I knew her.

MARTHA
That's only because she didn't like you.

WARRIOR
I'm sorry. You had a question for me? When you first came here, you wanted to ask me something.

MARIANNE
I forget. Mom?

MARTHA
You made me forget.

MARIANNE
I did not make you forget. You're getting old. You don't need my help. You can forget on your own.

MARTHA
I'm not listening to this. I'm leaving.

MARTHA exits as MARIANNE yells after her.

MARIANNE
Do you remember where our room is?

MARIANNE exits. THE WARRIOR is alone and returns to the window. He holds the sunglasses up to the sunlight, looking at his reflection.

WARRIOR
Hello, Ted Cardinal.

Scene Three

MARIANNE and MARTHA enter the cafeteria, arguing.

MARTHA

You want to know what your problem is? You don't have any respect for your elders!

MARIANNE

Well, my grey-haired sainted mother, you want to know what I think of that?

Both start sniffing the air.

MARIANNE

Is that curry?

MARTHA

And beaver. What an odd mixture.

MARIANNE

And that smells like fish, pickerel I think.

MARTHA

Yes, but mixed with something. I can't quite make it out.

MARIANNE

Peanut butter. I just got a weird feeling in the pit of my stomach and I don't think it's hunger.

AMOS appears at the doorway to the kitchen, looking a little messy and dishevelled.

MARIANNE

Amos, what are you doing in there?

AMOS

Having a nervous breakdown. It seems you can't fry whole wheat bannock in a skillet using just Pam.

MARTHA

Why would any sane man try?

AMOS

The same reason any sane man would do anything stupid. A woman.

MARTHA

Your little friend?

AMOS

Please, not now.I have to rethink the dinner menu. Have you seen the Warrior Who Never Sleeps?

MARIANNE

I think he's napping.

AMOS

I knew I shouldn't have listened to Summer. Her recipes aren't working. I should have went with my gut instinct. (*patting his belly*) And let me tell you, I have a lot of gut instinct.

MARIANNE

What are you making in there?

AMOS

The culinary equivalent of Frankenstein. I'm a man of pride. I take pride in my work. I can't serve this food. I don't know what to do.

MARIANNE

Can we help?

AMOS

I don't see how.

MARIANNE

Mom?

MARTHA
A man in the kitchen always made me nervous. Now I know why. A pretty face can turn a man's head but not a woman's when she's in the kitchen and knows what she's doing. When I cook, that kitchen belongs to me and Lord have mercy on those that enter my kingdom, for they walk through the valley of the shadow of Martha.

MARIANNE
Amen to that.

MARTHA
Amos, you got some money?

AMOS
Yes.

MARTHA
Give it to my daughter. Marianne, we need about thirty pounds of roast beef, two sacks of potatoes. Some corn, peas, lots of butter. You know the rest. Better pick up some salad fixings too. And some mayonnaise.

MARIANNE
We might need some desserts.

MARTHA
Good idea. Get some pies and cakes. You got the fixings for some real bannock in there?

AMOS
Of course.

MARIANNE
I'll be back in ... hopefully half an hour. I may even know where to dig up some fish. See ya soon.

MARIANNE rushes out.

MARTHA

This looks like a good strong table. Bring the flour and baking powder out here. We can get the bannock going.

MARTHA starts cleaning off the table in preparation. AMOS doesn't move.

MARTHA

Well, you waitin' for elves to do it for us? Move it!

AMOS rushes into the kitchen.

MARTHA

That's one thing about these Mohawk men, they always gotta wait for women to tell 'em to do things.

AMOS comes running about half way back when:

MARTHA

(*yelling*) Don't forget the salt.

AMOS turns around and disappears again for a few seconds, then reappears carrying all the ingredients. MARTHA starts laying them out on the table. For the rest of this scene, they are making bannock.

MARTHA

You work on one batch. I'll work on another. Is the oven preheated?

AMOS rushes back into the kitchen.

MARTHA

And he calls himself a cook. What kind of self-respecting cook doesn't have his oven ready and waiting?

AMOS returns to the table and struggles to catch up with the fast moving MARTHA.

MARTHA

It will be close but we should make it under the wire.

AMOS

Thank you. I wasn't expecting this. I'm usually very well-organized.

MARTHA

The Good Lord teaches us to help those who can't help themselves.

AMOS

Was he talking about me?

MARTHA

Why, were your ears burning?

AMOS

Hey, be careful there. You're getting flour on your dress.

AMOS hands her an apron. There is something in the pocket making it hit MARTHA on the leg.

MARTHA

Thank you. ... ouch! Something in the pocket hit me.

She fishes around in the pocket and pulls out a small can.

MARTHA

Spam? Why do you have a can of Spam in your apron pocket?

AMOS grabs the Spam, quickly hiding it.

AMOS

Shh, don't wave it about. If Summer sees it, she'll take it away from me.

MARTHA

Why?

AMOS

She doesn't want me eating canned meat. Says it's very bad for me. Evidently, Spam is evil.

MARTHA

That's her problem. She doesn't know what she's missing. I like canned meat.

AMOS

You like something evil?

MARTHA

Evil is in the eye of the beholder.

AMOS

Evil as it may be, I have a fondness for it. We call it government meat. It got us through some hard times. In a way, a good can of meat kind of makes me feel nostalgic.

MARTHA

So, are you a fried, baked, or raw man?

AMOS

Fried, with potatoes. Though I can eat it either way. I'm spambidextrous that way.

MARTHA

I remember my family keeping whole boxes of unlabelled cans in the basement. My father had to distribute it to everybody else in the village. It sure got us through some hard times.

AMOS

It may not be the most nutritious food, but it has a few more vitamins than starvation.

MARTHA

I prefer my meat sliced directly from the can. Marianne has the taste for it but my son Andrew can't stand it. God knows they had enough of it when they were in my belly. Times sure change.

AMOS

But not this stuff. I think this can could probably out
live us. Someday I hope to be buried in a Spam can. In
a hundred years time when they dig me up, it will sure
give them anthropologists something to think about.
(*conspiratorially*) Hey, want a slice?

MARTHA

What?! Right here? Right now?

AMOS

Hey, I won't tell if you won't.

MARTHA

Crack it open.

> *AMOS begins to open the can of Spam. He cuts his hand
> on the jagged metal.*

AMOS

Jesus!

> *He gets a hard look from MARTHA.*

AMOS

(*singing*) " ... loves me this I know. For the Bible tells
me so." Another one of my favorite hymns.

> *She finishes opening the can, slices off two wedges, and
> offers one to him. She takes the other.*

AMOS

It's not often you get to have a nice conversation about
canned meat.

MARTHA

Kids just don't know how to talk these days. (*toasting*)
To bannock and Spam.

AMOS

It's not just for breakfast anymore.

> *They both eat their slices.*

MARTHA
Where's your friend?

AMOS
If you are talking about Summer, I gave her the
afternoon off. She wasn't herself.

MARTHA
Teething pains?

MARTHA realizes she's ruining the moment.

MARTHA
That was rude. I shouldn't have said that.

AMOS
What is your problem?

MARTHA
Just being a silly old fool. Foolishness is not just a
pastime of the young. I'm sure she's a very nice girl ...
woman. Next time I see her I will tell her that.

Beat.

AMOS
She drives me up the wall.

MARTHA
I'm sorry to hear that. That can be a problem in a
relationship.

AMOS
And I'm not a young man anymore. Not to mention
my parents aren't too fond of an energetic young lady
like Summer.

MARTHA
Your parents! They still alive?

AMOS
Their names are Mother Nature and Father Time.
Kinda demanding too, as far as parents go. For a while

I was rebelling against their authority like all children do, but in the end, you can only say no to your parents for so long before they reach out and cuff you on the side of the head. And Summer has just about made me reach the end of their tolerance, especially Father Time. I'm afraid of being grounded. 'Cause when Father Time grounds you, the emphasis is on the word "ground." Oh I'm sorry, would you like another slice?

MARTHA
    Yes, please.

    AMOS cuts her off another slice and hands it to her. Their fingers touch and the moment is held. They realize something is happening. It scares them.

MARTHA
    Back to the bannock.

AMOS
    Yeah, back to the salt mines. Pass the salt. For my bannock. It needs ... salt.

    They continue on in silence, stealing quick glances from each other.

Scene Four

*Lights up on a woman sitting in the commons room,
looking out the window. She is SUMMER but dressed very
differently. She is now Agnes Ducharme and dressed
appropriately. She is talking to herself.*

SUMMER

Agnes Ducharme. Agnes Ducharme. Agnes Ducharme.

*A few seconds later, THE WARRIOR WHO NEVER SLEEPS,
enters the room. Except this time, he is Ted Cardinal, his
old self, dressed appropriately. He too feels somewhat
different and uncomfortable as he pours himself a coffee.
He sits, a fair distance from SUMMER. They are quiet.
Occasionally they look at each other and offer up a
hesitant smile.*

SUMMER

Excuse me, do you know what time the social begins?

WARRIOR

Um yes, when the sun travels ... about five o'clock.

SUMMER

Thank you.

They are silent again.

WARRIOR

Is this your first social?

SUMMER

No. I've been to a few.

WARRIOR

Me too.

Silence.

WARRIOR

I like socials.

99

SUMMER
   Me too.

WARRIOR
   My name is ... Ted. Ted Cardinal.

SUMMER
   I'm Agnes Ducharme. Pleased to meet you.

      Silence.

SUMMER
   I'm French.

WARRIOR
   I like *Star Trek.*

SUMMER
   I'm sorry but I never watch the show much. Except for that episode where the captain lost his memory and became a First Nations person.

WARRIOR
   The Paradise Syndrome. Third Season. The Indians were a combination of Delaware, Navaho and Mohican. He was called Kirok in that episode 'cause he lost his memory. (*pause*) It was directed by Jud Taylor.

SUMMER
   Oh. Thank you for sharing that.

WARRIOR
   I hope I'm not bothering you. I just have some time to kill till the feast. I thought I'd have a coffee. Would you like one?

SUMMER
   That would be nice. Just milk please.

      THE WARRIOR makes her coffee.

SUMMER
   Thank you.

WARRIOR
    The Klingons have their own form of coffee. It's
    called …

SUMMER
    Yes?

WARRIOR
    No. Never mind. It doesn't matter. I'm a neek again.
    I'd hoped I'd forgotten all this useless stuff. But I'll be
    cursed with *Star Trek* trivia till the day I travel the path
    … I mean die … I mean.. I'd better be going.

    THE WARRIOR gets up to leave but SUMMER stops him.

SUMMER
    What's wrong? You seem upset.

WARRIOR
    My life is so confusing. I'm not who you think I am. I'm
    not who I think I am. I don't know who I am.

SUMMER
    It's okay. I understand.

WARRIOR
    How could you?

SUMMER
    Trust me. I do.

WARRIOR
    You do?

SUMMER
    Yes.

WARRIOR
    In Klingon yes is translated as "hislah." In Cree it's …

SUMMER
    A'ha—tapwe'.

WARRIOR
You speak Cree?

SUMMER
A little bit. But I'll shut up now.

WARRIOR
No. Don't. It sounds nice. Tell me about yourself. In Cree.

SUMMER
I'd rather not.

WARRIOR
Why not?

SUMMER
It's too complicated to go into. It would just be false. It would be a lie.

WARRIOR
How can talking Cree be a lie?

Through the open door in the background, the PROFESSOR and AMOS can be seen walking by. AMOS stops when he spots SUMMER. He overhears.

SUMMER
All my life I have searched for a guide in my quest to understand the aboriginal spirit, although I do not look it, I am one sixty-fourth First Nations. I know, you are stunned. But I must face reality and accept my dominant heritage. I don't know if you can understand my dilemma but I always felt a day would come when a teacher who shared my curiosity and thirst for indigenous knowledge, would cross my path. I hunger for someone who shares my desire for a Native union of souls. I thought I had found him but though his spirit is honest and proud, he is not the one I search for. So after much personal wandering, I do not believe

there is such a person and I do believe the world is a far less interesting place for it. Maybe someday the Creator will see the need for such a being.

A pensive AMOS is pulled away by the impatient PROFESSOR.

SUMMER
Oh listen to me going on. I must be boring you. I'd better be going. It's been a pleasure, Mr. Cardinal.

SUMMER gets up and begins to leave the room. THE WARRIOR stands quickly, his arm raised in a fist.

WARRIOR
Free Leonard Peltier!

SUMMER stops in her tracks, mesmerized by THE WARRIOR's cry. She turns and races him, slowly raising her arm in a fist.

SUMMER
Oka forever!

They both feel the magnetism. Pheromones are released. Somewhere off in the distance, a coyote howls.

Scene Five

AMOS is sitting rather stiffly in PROFESSOR SAVAGE's office. But his mind is elsewhere.

SAVAGE

... and that's why I ended up doing my post-graduate work in Fiji, studying Polynesian erotic carvings. All in all, a most exciting field of study, don't you think?

AMOS doesn't respond.

SAVAGE

That's odd. Most people enjoy my Polynesian erotic carving stories. Do I have your attention, sir?

AMOS

I'm sorry. I was just thinking. You just never know how things are going to turn out. As long as you live, life can always throw you a curve. Be careful what you ask for, you might just get it. Old proverbs can be true ones, can't they?

SAVAGE

I suppose. It would help if I knew what you were talking about.

AMOS

No use crying over spilled milk. Another useful proverb. But a bird in the hand is worth two in the bush also comes to mind. You can't teach an old dog new tricks ... No, I don't like that one.

SAVAGE

Is this in any way relevant to the interview?

AMOS

What interview? Oh, sorry. My mind was a little occupied. This sex thing of yours huh?

SAVAGE
Just make yourself feel comfortable.

AMOS
Comfortable? I feel like I'm in the principal's office.
You don't got a strap in that drawer, do you?

SAVAGE
No, just a New Guinean penis sheath.

AMOS
Got one. Look, can we keep this short. I've got a whole
mess of cooking to finish before the big feast tonight.
Everything is in the oven and I have to be there when
the timer goes off. Somebody should be there. I have
to be there. Seems nobody else is gonna be there. Why
should anybody want to be there ...

SAVAGE
Ah, Native existentialism.

AMOS
Oh never mind me. Mind's rattling around a bit with
everything happening. Say, Professor, you should come
to the social. There might be some horny Indians there
for you to talk to.

SAVAGE
Thank you. I'll try. Now, Mr. ...

AMOS
Call me Amos.

SAVAGE
Amos, I understand you are a widower.

AMOS
Going on nine years now. Helen was her name. The
light of my creation, the passion in my soul. We had

five beautiful daughters together till her life fire went out.

SAVAGE

I'm sorry to hear that. Have you dated much since then?

AMOS

Recently I've been dabbling.

SAVAGE

Dabbling is good. Now I saw you earlier with a companion.

Beat.

SAVAGE

At least that's what you led me to believe.

AMOS

Summer is more than a dabble. Quite a handful in fact. More than a handful. I have never met anyone with so much enthusiasm, so many questions and such a zest for life. Lotta zest there. A whole whack of zest. Perhaps too much zest.

SAVAGE

Do I detect a note of dissatisfaction?

AMOS

That's between Summer and me.

SAVAGE

I understand. But has there been anybody else of interest?

AMOS

You flatter me. A man my age doesn't generate much interest, Professor. You see, we Elders are in an unusual position. We're respected and honoured by the community. But with that admiration, comes a certain amount of expectations.

SAVAGE
What do you mean by expectations?

AMOS
Maybe I should have said limitations. Romance and sex aren't exactly expected in an Elder. It makes us too … human. A man my age and position isn't supposed to be lonely, or have needs. I'm supposed to be a needless man. Some sort of a Zen thing.

SAVAGE
Interesting, and by "needs" you mean …

AMOS
Geez, with all these letters behind your name, you'd think you'd be a little quicker on the ball. I'm talking about the need for companionship. Being a widower for nine years can be an awful lonely profession. Being an Elder is wonderful but that too can be lonely. Young people have so many questions and I'm supposed to have all the answers. I spend most of my time as a reference library. Sometimes I just need somebody to talk to who doesn't have any questions. I know I come from a different era, but there must be somebody else out there who knows who Red Foley is.

SAVAGE
Wasn't he a country singer?

AMOS
You doing anything later, Professor?

SAVAGE
I take it Summer doesn't quite suit your needs.

AMOS

Did I tell you she once beaded my underwear? Yeah!
Beaded a medicine wheel right onto my Hanes. God,
now that was truly an indescribable feeling. But that
wonderful, lovely and bright woman, who was born
when I was potty training my third daughter, thinks the
McCarthy era refers to the Beatles.

SAVAGE

Perhaps you should look elsewhere?

AMOS

Professor, once depreciation is taken into account, I'm
not much of a buy. Not when there are new models on
the lot. But still, life goes on, doesn't it?

SAVAGE

Another proverb?

AMOS

I've got another one for you. Physician, heal thy self.

SAVAGE

I am not ill.

*AMOS reaches onto his desk and picks up a framed
photograph.*

AMOS

Either this is a photograph of your cat, or your wife has
pointy ears and needs a shave.

SAVAGE

My relationship with my cat is not pertinent to this
interview.

AMOS

You spend hours talking to people about dating and
sex, and you have a picture of a cat on your desk. At

least the kisses I got when I came home didn't smell of tuna.

SAVAGE

"Didn't." Past tense. Interesting.

AMOS

Good-bye. Present tense. I don't want to make your cat jealous.

AMOS gets up angrily and leaves. The PROFESSOR grabs his framed photograph.

SAVAGE

This isn't even my cat. This is my sister's cat.

He reaches over to the opposite side of his desk, to another framed picture.

SAVAGE

Now this is Beowulf.

The PROFESSOR realizes he is holding two framed pictures of cats in his hands. The realization is unsettling.

SAVAGE

Maybe I do need to get out more.

Scene Six

The cafeteria. MARIANNE is putting together the final touches for the salad as MARTHA enters.

MARIANNE
Hey Mom, there you are. The roast beef should be ready ...

MARTHA
Is Amos here?

MARIANNE
No. He's off being interviewed by that Professor guy.

MARTHA
Good.

MARTHA disappears into the kitchen. SUMMER and THE WARRIOR wander in, obviously in love.

MARIANNE
Oh God, here comes both ad and nauseum.

SUMMER
Hey Marianne, I don't suppose Amos is around?

MARIANNE
No but isn't all this cooking stuff supposed to be your work?

SUMMER
I am so sorry but I've been going through something of an identity crisis.

MARIANNE
Yeah yeah, we had this conversation. I thought you wanted to "embrace your new reality."

SUMMER
It was a false reality. This is my new reality.

WARRIOR
Today is a good day to find the first day of the rest of your life ... or something like that.

SUMMER
Isn't he magnificent?

MARIANNE
I'm in awe. How does Amos feel about this?

SUMMER
Amos is a wise and compassionate man. He knows the ways of the heart do not always run smoothly.

WARRIOR
I mean no disrespect to our Elder but we are meant for each other. That is the path the Creator has set. Make it so, eh Babe? We must honour it.

AMOS enters.

MARIANNE
I'd get honouring if I were you.

WARRIOR
Oh oh, Captain on the Bridge.

SUMMER
Amos, I ...

AMOS
I know.

SUMMER
How could you?

AMOS
I'm an Elder. I'm supposed to be all-knowing, remember?

SUMMER
Have I hurt you?

AMOS

With a hundred people here to feed and only two hours to finish, I don't have time to be hurt. But I do have the time to wish you the best. My heart sings for you. Don't be so surprised, Summer, you were and are my heart's delight and I truly mean this. So when I say go off and be happy, believe me. Life threw us together for a period of time and the only true measure of the quality of that time is if you leave with more happy memories than bad ones.

SUMMER

Oh Amos, I have lots of happy memories. You have helped in making me the woman I am and I thank you for your guidance and love. I hope I have left you with some happy memories.

AMOS

Quite a few, young lady. And some pulled muscles. Be strong and enjoy your journey. You deserve it. Warrior That Never Sleeps, come here.

THE WARRIOR approaches.

AMOS

You have quite a woman there, young man.

WARRIOR

You're not upset?

AMOS

Everything in this world has a life expectancy, people, ideas, plants. I am a little sad but I am a realist. Her happiness is more important. Take good care of Summer and get yourself a good health plan.

WARRIOR
Cool. The words you speak honour us. I will take good care of Summer. I guess that makes two to beam up, Babe.

AMOS
Now go off and be young.

SUMMER
Thank you Amos.

SUMMER runs up and kisses AMOS on the cheek. Then SUMMER and THE WARRIOR exit.

MARIANNE
You're a very forgiving man.

AMOS
I have five girls. They taught me that the hard way. How's the dinner coming?

MARIANNE
Pretty good. The salad is almost finished and Mom is in the kitchen ...

MARTHA enters the room and runs into AMOS. They stare at each other, uncomfortable.

MARIANNE
So Mom, we still gotta slice the beef and mash the potatoes and ...

AMOS
I'll go check the potatoes.

AMOS exits.

MARIANNE
... and the vegetables are ...

MARTHA
I'll be right back.

MARTHA exits out a different door.

MARIANNE

... just about done. (*loudly*) Anybody still here? I'm just about done the salad and I'm not even supposed to be making salad. Again I'm stuck alone in the kitchen. This is the reason I got divorced and I'm running out of people to divorce!

AMOS sticks his head out of the kitchen.

AMOS

Is your mother gone?

MARIANNE

Yeah, so?

AMOS enters carrying a big pot of cooked potatoes.

AMOS

Good. I could use your help mashing the potatoes.

MARIANNE

My mother should be back in a second. She can help too as soon as ...

AMOS

She's coming back? Maybe I should put on a clean shirt or something. When is she coming back?

MARIANNE

Whenever I'm allowed to finish a goddamn sentence without somebody leaving the room or interrupting me! What is going on here? What is it between you two and ...

The reality starts to click in.

MARIANNE

Oh my god, oh my god ... You like my mother! You got the hots for my mommy! Oh my god, that's disgusting!

AMOS

I do not. You behave yourself.

MARIANNE

I don't believe this. And Mom ... she likes you too! She has to. It all makes sense!

AMOS

She does?

MARIANNE

No! No! This isn't right. You stay away from my mommy! You're both old. Grow up!

He starts to mash the potatoes savagely.

MARIANNE

Amos, my mother hasn't had a date in forty years. Forty years! Hasn't kissed a man since my father. This may be a regular thing for you Mohawk guys but please, leave my mother out of this. She'd have a better chance of operating the space shuttle than going out on a date.

AMOS is silent.

MARIANNE

Don't clam up on me now, Amos. This is serious business. Do you like my mother or am I imagining it?

AMOS is still silent.

MARIANNE

Silence is the best companion of those in love.

AMOS

That's pretty good. Where'd you learn that?

MARIANNE

Oprah. So it's true.

AMOS

I barely know your mother.

MARIANNE
But you'd like to know her more?

AMOS
She seems like a very lovely woman.

MARIANNE
You would think so, wouldn't you?

AMOS
I mean, any woman who likes a big helping of canned meat ...

MARIANNE
Spare me the Mohawk metaphors, this is my mother you're talking about.

AMOS
Do you think it could work? I'm so out of practice at this kind of thing. Summer sort of came gift-wrapped. But when I was young, that was a different story. One kiss and I could tell you how many fillings a girl had.

MARIANNE
I'm sure some people think that is kinda cute but ... I didn't think people your age still thought about stuff like this. I mean, you guys are old.

AMOS
I have to do something. I'm running out of church hymns. As a Longhouse guy I only know so many.

MARIANNE
But you guys are old!

AMOS
What do you think? Ojibway and Mohawk? Christian and Longhouse? Can it work?

MARIANNE
But you guys are old!

AMOS

Will you quit saying that like it's a bad thing. Being old isn't bad.

MARIANNE

You're right ... you're right ... This is just so weird. Really weird. How does Mom feel about all this?

AMOS

I thought you said she liked me.

MARIANNE

I was guessing. Assuming. I don't believe I'm having this conversation.

AMOS

This is silly. Enough of this foolishness. Thank you, Marianne for your help, but it's time I concentrate on what I'm getting paid for. It's cooking time.

AMOS disappears into the kitchen.

MARIANNE

My mom and a Mohawk man? Who knew an Elders' conference could turn into a singles' bar?

Scene Seven

The social, in the commons room. Drum music is playing and people are milling about, waiting. AMOS is bringing out small sandwiches, and MARTHA stays at the opposite side of the room.

MARIANNE
So, how is the research going?

SAVAGE
Not as quickly as I'd hoped. Some of the answers I've been getting have been quite enigmatic. The concepts of "snagging" and playing "the snake and the donut" seem unusually unique.

MARIANNE
Professor, those things you learn by doing, not asking.

SAVAGE
But I'm supposed to be an objective observer. By participating in the research, it could adversely affect the results.

MARIANNE
Do you cook?

SAVAGE
As a matter of fact I do. What has that to ...

MARIANNE
Do you use a cookbook?

SAVAGE
Sometimes.

MARIANNE
Do you just follow the recipe or do you cook by taste?

SAVAGE
Both. That's not a fair comparison.

MARIANNE
Neither are apples and oranges but both have a place on my table.

SUMMER comes running up to the PROFESSOR.

SUMMER
Professor! Professor!

SAVAGE
Excellent, I was hoping to run into you. We must schedule your interview. How are you fixed for ...

SUMMER
That's just it. I'm sorry but I won't be here after the social.

MARIANNE
You're gonna miss the conference?

SUMMER
I know and it saddens me. But Ted and I are off to this aboriginal *Star Trek* convention.

SAVAGE
There's such a thing?

SUMMER
It's all the rage and as luck would have it, there's one this weekend! What are the chances! It's called Dances With Worfs—A Look at Planet Claims in the 24th Century. We're leaving tonight.

MARIANNE
Wow. You two work quickly.

SUMMER
It's just been such a special day. Sometimes it feels like I just don't know where I'm gonna end up. If I don't see you before I leave, thank you both. Gotta go. Au revoir.

MARIANNE

You know, if they begin to have kids, I may move to Iceland.

SAVAGE

I've been to Iceland. It's quite a wonderful place.

MARIANNE

It's a date.

From a distance, MARTHA waves her hand at MARIANNE, trying to get her attention. MARIANNE approaches.

MARTHA

Marianne, Amos keeps looking at me. I want you to ask him why?

MARIANNE

Oh come on Mother, you know why. Blow the dust out of your cleavage and go talk to the man. He's a hunka-hunka-burnin'-Mohawk if you ask me.

MARTHA

You're just being silly.

MARIANNE

I'm a lot of things, Mom, but I don't run away from people who just want to talk with me. It's allowed, you know.

MARTHA

It makes me uncomfortable.

MARIANNE

Then get comfortable.

MARTHA

That's easy for you to say. It's been too long for me.

MARIANNE

Try being adaptable. You were born during World War Two, since then you've seen people land on the moon, Native women get their status back, Oka, the Spice Girls, going up and talking to that man is not a major crisis in the big scheme of life. And speaking of comfortable, this is not a discussion I am comfortable having with my mother. I keep getting these visual images ...

She shudders.

MARIANNE

Now, if you will excuse me, there is another Kakina woman in this room who isn't afraid to get back up on that horse. I just hope I remembered to bring my riding crop.

MARIANNE wanders away. AMOS comes closer, near SUMMER and THE WARRIOR, dropping off some food. MARTHA makes a half-hearted attempt to approach him but backs off, too frightened.

WARRIOR

What are these?

AMOS

Oh, some marinated venison on a wedge of whole wheat toast.

SUMMER

Hey, that's one of my recipes!

AMOS

It's quite lovely. Everybody's been talking about it.

WARRIOR

It is very good. The spirit of the deer will be honoured.

AMOS
   I'm glad for the deer.

SUMMER
   Do you need help?

AMOS
   No, I'm fine.

   AMOS and MARTHA run into each other, share a nervous
   moment then move away. MARTHA quickly takes a seat
   while AMOS disappears back into the kitchen.

MARTHA
   This is ridiculous.

   The PROFESSOR joins her.

SAVAGE
   Hello, Mrs. Kakina. I was hoping we'd have the chance
   to talk again.

MARTHA
   Uh huh.

SAVAGE
   I realize this is not the best atmosphere in which to
   conduct an interview but while we're here ...

MARTHA
   You are a persistent little white man, aren't you?

   The music changes when an Iroquoian water drum song
   is played.

SUMMER
   It's the Alligator Dance. I love this dance.

   She quickly grabs THE WARRIOR and they start the dance.
   The PROFESSOR takes out a pen and paper.

SAVAGE
   I believe we left off discussing ...

As the PROFESSOR is writing things down, MARTHA
waves to MARIANNE to get her attention.

MARTHA
Marianne!

She then points to the occupied PROFESSOR. MARIANNE
understands and makes her way over to the PROFESSOR
and MARTHA.

MARIANNE
Hey Mom, mind if I borrow tall, white and handsome
for a moment?

MARTHA
Take him.

MARIANNE
Hey, you wanna dance?

SAVAGE
I'm flattered but ...

MARTHA
I thought it was rude to refuse the woman?

MARIANNE
Feel like insulting all six different Nations before
dinner?

SAVAGE
Very well, but I don't suppose you know very much
about the socio-dynamic implications of trans-
cultural ...

MARIANNE
Oh shut up and dance.

MARIANNE practically drags the PROFESSOR out onto the
dance floor.

They begin to Alligator Dance. MARTHA is left alone,
watching from her seat. Pretty soon AMOS enters from the
kitchen with more food. He is pleased with the song and
happily watches the others dance. Then he spots MARTHA
and quickly begins working again.

MARTHA spots him.

MARTHA

Martha Kakina, you are a silly old fool.

She marches right over to AMOS, grabs his arm and pulls
him out to the dance floor. At first AMOS is stunned by the
gesture. But it quickly becomes obvious that MARTHA
doesn't know any of the steps and AMOS has to go from
being surprised to being the instructor. Before long,
MARTHA has the beat and all the cast members are
joyously dancing the Alligator Dance.

[NOTE: For those unfamiliar with the Alligator Dance,
it's a line dance where couples, with arms linked, follow
the movements of the lead dancers and wind their way
around the dance floor in a circular pattern. It is a fun
social dance.]

One by one, the dancers disappear off stage as they follow
the lead dancers. All is quiet for a moment, then a knock
can be heard several times at a door. There is no response.
Slowly the door opens and a young, pretty woman enters.
It is MISS INDIAN WORLD, complete with sash, alone, on
stage. She enters hesitantly, looking around.

MISS INDIAN WORLD

Hello? Is anybody here? I'm Miss Indian World. Hello?
(*silence, then pathetically*) Hello?

[NOTE: For this character, a person from the local Native
community should be enlisted for this momentary walk on.]

Scene Eight

We are back at the lecture hall. PROFESSOR SAVAGE is giving a summary of his experiences at the conference. He looks a little worse for wear. He may even have a hickey.

SAVAGE

So, in conclusion, let me add that despite my repeated efforts to obtain valuable raw research material for this presentation, I was unable to crack the silence that exists amongst these unique people. As a result, we now know less about them than when the project began, I'm sorry to say. I did, however, find out that Ojibway women like being tickled. Suffice to say, that will not be in my final report to the SSHRC office. And also, if anybody in the room is interested in taking possession of a cat, I'm in the process of giving mine away. I have a feeling I won't be home much to look after him.

The PROFESSOR takes out a can of Spam from his coat pocket and proceeds to open it. As he talks, he slices off a chunk and eats it.

SAVAGE

Nevertheless, it is my sincere and honest recommendation that I be allowed to continue in my important research, and that I be allowed to delve deeper, ever so much deeper, into the complex and mysterious world of the Erotic Aboriginal, and I will dedicate myself to the unravelling of this cryptic and unseen sub-culture. Or die trying. And now if you'll excuse me, I've got a date.

The PROFESSOR wanders off stage, still eating the Spam. Lights go down.

END